50s WEST

EXETER TO PENZANCE

ROGER SIVITER

Front cover: At mid-morning on Sunday 8 July 1984, Class 50 No 50048 *Dauntless* approaches Dawlish Warren station with an empty coaching stock train from Westbury bound for Paignton and returning holidaymakers. On the right hand side is the former GWR signal box and in the distance some of the many semaphore signals that controlled the area.

Christina Siviter

Back cover: No 50018 *Resolution*, in Network South-East livery, is seen near Restormel, just to the north of Lostwithiel, in charge of the 11.45 Paddington to Penzance train, which is due to arrive at the south-westerly terminus at 17.25, 5 hours 40 minutes for the 305 mile journey. 28 August 1987.

Roger Siviter

Right: In brilliant summer sunshine on Sunday 16 August 1987, No 50048, this time in Network South-East livery, emerges from the Parson & Clerk tunnel, situated between Dawlish and Teignmouth, with the 08.15 Birmingham New Street to Paignton train. Note the platelayer/workman's hut on the left hand side as a reminder of GWR days.   *Roger Siviter*

© Roger Siviter 2001
Published by Great Bear Publishing
34 Shannon Way, Evesham WR11 3FF Tel: 01386 765134

ISBN 0-9541150-0-7

Designed and produced by Viners Wood Associates Tel: 01452 812813
Printed in England by Ian Allan Ltd, Surrey.

Above: Our journey proper starts at Cowley Bridge junction, one mile to the north of Exeter St Davids station, where on the morning of Saturday 30 July 1983 English Electric Class 50 No 50036 *Victorious* heads for Paignton with the 06.53 holiday train from Oxford. The line on the left is the former Southern Railway route to Plymouth, now terminating at Meldon Quarry, with the Barnstaple line branching off at Coleford Junction, situated to the west of Crediton. At this time, the whole area was controlled by semaphore signalling, but within two years, this would change with the advent of the Exeter power box. Note the delightful little waterfall just to the left of the splendid signal box, and on the right hand side the familiar landmark of the Cowley Bridge pub. *Christina Siviter*

Opposite: Looking round from the previous picture, we see No 50007 as it heads east through Cowley Bridge on 7 July 1984 with the 17.45 from Paignton to Paddington. This locomotive was originally named *Hercules*, but in the early 1980s was refurbished in GWR green, complete with cast number plate, and named *Sir Edward Elgar* after the former GWR Castle Class 4-6-0 No 7005. It is now owned by the 'Class 40 Appeal'. Like the previous picture, semaphore signals were still in control but only just, because as can be seen colour lights, etc. were being erected. *Christina Siviter*

Introduction

After their introduction in 1967, the English Electric 2700hp Class 50 locomotives worked on the London Midland Region, but by 1976 they were all to be found on the Western Region, mainly as a replacement for the Western Class hydraulic diesels, which were all withdrawn by 1977.

So for just over a decade until around 1989 these popular locomotives were to be seen working many of the principal trains between Paddington and Devon and Cornwall, and from Birmingham New Street to Paignton, Plymouth and Penzance.

At first, the class were to be seen in the standard BR blue livery, but with refurbishment in the early 1980s they were turned out in the very attractive 'large logo' livery which, coupled with the naming of the locomotives as well as the wonderful sound they emitted, made them very popular with traction enthusiasts. Later on, some members of the class were painted in Network South-East livery plus, of course, No 50007 in GWR green and No 50I49 (50049) in Railfreight grey.

This book is a tribute to these illustrious locomotives, with a journey by them on one of the most attractive routes in the British Isles, between Exeter and Penzance, and incidentally features each member of the class.

In compiling this book I should like to thank my wife Christina, Hugh Ballantyne, Joe Burr of the '50 Fund', Chris Holland of the 'Class 50 Society', and last but not least the railwaymen who make it all possible.

Roger Siviter
Evesham, 2001

50s WEST BIBLIOGRAPHY

Diesels in the Duchy by John Vaughan
　　Published by Ian Allan

Past and Present No 8 Devon by David Mitchell
　　Published by Past and Present Publishing

Past and Present No I7 Cornwall by David Mitchell
　　Published by Past and Present Publishing

50s in Devon and Cornwall by Roger Siviter
　　Published by Kingfisher/Runpast Publishing

We are now at the north end of Exeter St Davids station, where on one of the busiest days of the year, Saturday 30 July 1983, the first of the class No 50001 *Dreadnought*, still in the original blue livery, waits to leave platform six with the 09.35 Paignton to Paddington train. Through the signal gantry can be seen the fine-looking GWR signal box which also controlled the busy level crossing which is at the end of the platforms. *Roger Siviter*

Exeter locomotive shed (83C) was situated on the western side of the station and although the shed was closed in 1964, the area was used (and still used today) for refuelling and stabling diesel locomotives. On 18 February 1988, Class 50s No 50149 (formerly No 50049) *Defiance* in Railfreight grey and No 50017 *Royal Oak* in Network South-East livery await their next turn of duty in Exeter shed yard. No 50049 has been preserved by 'The Class 50 Society'. *Roger Siviter*

I think that Class 50s look impressive at any time but perhaps none more so than at night. *Monarch*, No 50010, certainly looks impressive as it waits to leave Exeter St Davids station on the evening of 30 October 1984 with the 19.34 train to Waterloo. On the right hand side is an HST on a down Plymouth train.

Roger Siviter

No 50016 *Barham* looks a treat as it pulls out of the impressive former GWR
St Davids station and heads westwards with the 11.15 Birmingham New Street
to Penzance train on 26 April 1984. This train originated at Liverpool Lime
Street, departure time 09.20.   *Christina Siviter*

On 7 July 1984, No 50039 *Implacable* crosses over the River Exe as it leaves St Davids station with the 11.47 Birmingham New Street to Paignton train. To the left of the picture can be seen two Class 33 locomotives, Nos 33113 and 33014, on the empty stock of a Waterloo train, and behind the second and third carriages of the Paignton train, Exeter West signal box is clearly visible. Happily, this box has been preserved in working order at Crewe Heritage Centre. Dominating this busy scene is a fine example of a GWR bracket signal. Note the distant arm on the middle post is motor driven, the other two being fixed distants. Note also the pair of GWR elevated ground signals by the bracket post.

Christina Siviter

Some five miles west of Exeter, the line runs through Exminster which once boasted a station, but this was closed many years ago. On a sunny winter's afternoon (17 February 1988) No 50009 *Conqueror* approaches the site of Exminster station with the 14.15 Plymouth to Leeds van train. By this time, the signal box was obviously out of action, but it is still there to this day, presumably used as a store.

Roger Siviter

The refurbishment of the Class 50s took place between 1979 and the early 1980s, and one of the distinguishing marks of refurbishment was the addition of a central headlamp. At first, some were turned out in the old blue livery, and so in this picture of *Benbow* No 50012 the absence of the central headlight tells us that it is awaiting refurbishing. *Benbow* is seen at Starcross on the early morning of 18 August 1979 with the 07.10 Exeter to Plymouth train. *Hugh Ballantyne*

Brunel's pumping station at Starcross provides an historical backdrop for No 50040 *Centurion* (formerly *Leviathan*) as it hurries through the station on an inclement day with the 11.55 Penzance to Birmingham New Street, and then to Liverpool Lime Street. 2 September 1984. Note the station sign – Starcross for Exmouth ferry – the pier leading to the ferry terminal can be seen on the left hand side. Also, just above the second coach can be seen a bow window, from which ferry travellers could observe the arrival of the ferry. *Christina Siviter*

Above: Around a mile from Starcross, the line crosses over the picturesque Cockwood Harbour, where I suppose that over the last 50 years or so as many pictures have been taken as at any railway location in the UK. On the early evening of Sunday 23 August 1987, Class 50 No 50048 *Dauntless* crosses the harbour with the17.10 Paignton to Waterloo train. *Roger Siviter*

Opposite: On this south-westerly route from Exeter, the first contact with the 'seaside' is at Dawlish Warren, very popular with visitors and locals alike. On a warm and sunny Sunday in July 1984 (the 8th) No 50043 *Eagle* receives admiring glances from holidaymakers as it leaves Dawlish Warren station and heads for Dawlish with the 08.45 Cardiff to Paignton train. In the station can be seen an HST on the 08.35 Penzance to Paddington train. Note also the semaphore signals, the ex-GWR camping coaches and also the popular tea bar on the lower right hand side of the picture. *Christina Siviter*

The previous picture was taken from Langstone Rock and this picture, taken a few minutes later, shows an up train as it runs between the headland and Langstone Rock. The train is the 11.10 Paignton to Waterloo service hauled by No 50049 *Defiance*, then in 'large logo' livery. In the background can be seen the famous Devon coastal resort of Dawlish. Are the 'Hoover-bashers' in the front coach admiring the young lady as she enjoys an ice cream, or waving at the photographer?

Christina Siviter

On Sunday 23 August 1987, No 50009 *Conqueror* speeds past the red cliffs at Dawlish with the 11.15 Paignton to Waterloo train via Exeter Central and Salisbury, arriving at the London terminus at 15.48. One of the great joys of the south Devon coastal area if you are on holiday (or if you have lived there, as my wife and I did during 1987 and 1988) is the walk along the sea wall between Dawlish Warren and Dawlish, and also from the Parson & Clerk tunnel to Teignmouth.

Roger Siviter

After running through Dawlish, the line threads through a series of short tunnels before emerging into the photogenic location known as Horse Cove, formerly used in pre-war days by the GWR for publicity posters, etc. No 50039 *Implacable* is seen at Horse Cove on Saturday 15 August 1987 in charge of the 11.10 Paddington to Newquay train. 1987 was the last summer when the Class 50 locomotives worked trains to this popular Cornish seaside resort. The town of Dawlish and its beaches provide a suitable backdrop to this classic railway seascape.   *Roger Siviter*

Turning round from the previous scene, we see *Eagle*, No 50043, heading through Horse Cove on the afternoon of Tuesday 25 August 1987 with an up train of empty mineral wagons.

Roger Siviter

After Horse Cove, the line runs through the more lengthy Parson & Clerk tunnel (see frontispiece) and then after a mile or so along the sea wall swings inland to Teignmouth station, and then runs up beside the Teign estuary to the ancient market town of Newton Abbot. In brilliant summer sunshine, No 50038

Formidable leaves the skewbridge at Teignmouth and heads along the sea wall with the 09.24 Paignton to Birmingham New Street train on 7 July 1984.

Christina Siviter

The next picture, taken from Teignmouth dockyard on 14 February 1984, shows *Indomitable* (No 50026) as it runs under Shaldon bridge and approaches Teignmouth with the 11.38 Plymouth to Manchester train. Notice the old toll house (now in private ownership) above the fifth and sixth carriages. I well remember my first holiday in south Devon in the glorious summer of 1947, when the toll for crossing the bridge was one old penny. *Hugh Ballantyne*

Above: The next view was taken from Shaldon bridge itself, looking towards Teignmouth dockyard, and shows a brace of Class 50s heading up the Teign estuary with the 10.40 Paddington to Penzance train on 19 August 1984. The leading locomotive is No 50009 *Conqueror* together with *Collingwood*, No 50005.

Christina Siviter

Opposite: Looking round the other way, we see No 50021 *Rodney* glowing in the autumn sunshine as it approaches Shaldon bridge with the up Torbay Express – the 14.47 Paignton to Paddington train. By this time, this working was rostered for an HST, so this was obviously a rare occurrence. 16 October 1987.

Roger Siviter

Some five miles inland from Teignmouth is Newton Abbot where, on the evening of Saturday 7 September 1985, Class 50 No 50025 *Invincible* approaches platform one of the busy station with the 15.18 Birmingham New Street (13.25 ex Manchester Picadilly) to Paignton train. Framing the train is one of the station's gantry signals which, together with the signal boxes, would all disappear within the following two years. Also to the left of the signal box is the start of the freight-only line to Heathfield, from where the inland route to Exeter (Teign Valley line) left the branch line to Moreton Hampstead. Both lines closed in the 1960s.

Christina Siviter

On 7 July 1984, No 50032 *Courageous* waits to leave Newton Abbot station with the up car carrier train. From 1982 onwards, coaches were not attached to this train, passengers having to travel by normal service train. By 1984 it was unusual to find a Class 50 on this duty, Class 47s being the usual motive power.

No 50032's nameplate was unique in having a blue background instead of red. Note the fine-looking station buildings and GWR platform canopies.

Christina Siviter

Benbow, No 50012, heads westwards out of Newton Abbot with the 11.25 Birmingham-Penzance train on Wednesday 22 April 1987. This view showed the station area more or less how it had looked since the closure of the old steam shed (83A) in the 1960s, when a diesel MPD was built on its site (right hand side background). The colour light signal in front of the gantry gives an indication of things to come. In fact, within a few days of this picture being taken, work started on the removal of the signal boxes and semaphore signals, together with refurbishment of the track layout. Thankfully this signal gantry was preserved by the publishers David & Charles and re-erected by their offices, the edge of which can be seen on the extreme right hand side of the picture.

Christina Siviter

During 1983 and 1984, some of the Paddington to Penzance trains were loaded to fifteen coaches and nicknamed 'Jumbo' trains. One such working was the 14.45 Paddington to Penzance train seen here approaching Aller junction on 7 July 1984 with No 50009 in charge. Eight passenger stops, including seven minutes at Plymouth, were allowed for this train, which was scheduled to arrive in Penzance at 20.42. *Christina Siviter*

Aller junction was where the Paignton and Plymouth lines split. The layout was altered with the advent of colour light signalling, and the two sets of lines now simply diverge. This view at Aller was obviously taken before resignalling and shows the area when it was a true junction. Approaching the camera on 22 April 1987 is No 50027 *Lion*, in charge of the 13.58 Penzance to Bristol train.

At the rear of the train is the start of Dainton bank (1 in 41 at its steepest) while the line to Torquay and Paignton can be seen swinging away above the Plymouth line. The GWR signal box and neat-looking allotments (at one time a common sight on railway land) add to what is now an historic picture.

Roger Siviter

During their time in the south-west, the Class 50s worked regularly on Paignton trains, especially so on summer Saturdays. Once the trains had reached Paignton and discharged their passengers, the locomotives would take their empty coaching stock to Goodrington sidings (a few hundred yards from Paignton station) for stabling until their return workings. On Saturday 1 September 1984, No 50006 *Neptune* pulls out of Goodrington sidings with the ECS of the 15.35 Paignton to Bristol train, having worked in earlier with the 11.15 from Paddington. At the rear of the train is Peak Class locomotive No 45029 waiting its turn to leave the sidings with ECS for the 16.08 to Birmingham New Street. The line on the left is part of the Torbay Steam Railway line to Kingswear. *Christina Siviter*

We are now back on the line to Plymouth at Dainton tunnel, the summit of the lines from Newton Abbot and Totnes respectively. In pleasant spring sunshine No 50034 *Furious*, now in Network South-East livery, has just emerged from Dainton tunnel and is heading down the bank to Totnes with the 06.45 Swindon to Penzance train. The areas either side of the track were once filled with sidings. They also give some idea of the steepness of the gradient at this point – around 1 in 37/38. Notice also the very utilitarian-looking signal box. 23 April 1987.

Roger Siviter

When my wife and I lived in Newton Abbot around 1987/1988, we would often hear the 50s as they roared up Dainton bank, because these English Electric machines could make a terrific sound. This was certainly the case on 17 October 1987 when I photographed No 50020 *Revenge* as it roared up Dainton near Wrigwell Hill with the 14.15 Plymouth to Leeds parcels train. It had been audible more or less all the way from Totnes, some five miles away.

Roger Siviter

Left: The mediaeval town of Totnes is our next location as No 50008 *Thunderer* speeds through the station with the 09.45 Paddington to Plymouth train on Sunday 8 September 1985. In the background is a familiar landmark, the Unigate Creamery. Totnes is not only the start of Dainton bank to the east but also the start of the second of the three famous Devon banks, Rattery, which runs westwards from Totnes along the edge of Dartmoor with gradients as steep as 1 in 46. In steam days, banking engines from Newton Abbot shed were stabled at Totnes to assist heavy trains over the steep gradients. Totnes was also the junction for the picturesque branch line to Ashburton, which closed in 1962. It was reopened in the late 1960s as the Dart Valley Railway as far as Buckfastleigh, but without a passenger connection with Totnes station. *Christina Siviter*

Right: Resplendent in 'large logo' livery, together with a silver roof, No 50001 is seen at the foot of Rattery bank, just about to enter Totnes station and make a stop with the 09.50 Plymouth to Paignton train, on 2 September 1984. If you look at the rear of the train, you get some idea of the steepness of Rattery bank. Note also the variety of signalling.

Christina Siviter

Sometimes you would find Class 50s on rather mundane duties such as on a bright 22 December 1987 as No 50002 *Superb* ambles down the eastern end of Rattery bank near Totnes station with a ballast train. The train then stopped in the middle road of the station for reballasting work to take place.

Roger Siviter

No 50014 *Warspite* has just run through South Brent (formerly the junction for the branch to Kingsbridge) and heads westwards towards Plymouth with the 09.14 Brighton to Penzance train. The date is 7 September 1985. In the background is Brent Moor, part of Dartmoor National Park. *Warspite* was one of the earliest 50s to be withdrawn, being taken out of service in December 1987.

Hugh Ballantyne

Opposite: Our next picture is still on the edge of Dartmoor, near Ivybridge, and shows one of the few Class 50s to carry miniature snow ploughs, No 50024 *Vanguard*, as it heads westwards on the evening of 13 April 1988 with a train of concrete sleepers.
Roger Siviter

Above: The third great Devon railway bank is Hemerdon, which runs roughly from Tavistock Junction on the outskirts of Plymouth to Hemerdon Siding, a distance of around four miles, with gradients as steep as 1 in 41/42. On Sunday 1 September 1985, No 50026 *Indomitable* tops Hemerdon bank in fine style and passes Hemerdon Siding with the 11.35 Penzance to Paddington train.
Christina Siviter

By kind permission of BR, these next two views were taken at Plymouth Laira Traction and Maintenance depot, on 3 April 1985. The first view shows Class 50 No 50046 *Ajax* with a newly painted black roof, inside the maintenance depot at Laira. In the second view taken at the depot's yard, No 50041 *Bulwark* waits to move into the maintenance depot, while on the main line No 50019 *Ramillies* heads eastwards with an empty stock train. This diesel depot, etc. was opened in 1962 and was built near the site of the steam shed which closed around 1964.

Top right: Roger Siviter
Bottom right: Christina Siviter

Opposite: On 28 May 1985, No 50029 *Renown* runs by the River Plym as it approaches Plymouth Laira with the 13.40 Paddington-Penzance train. Behind the train can be seen the A38 trunk road which now bypasses the city of Plymouth and runs directly to the Saltash road bridge. Beyond the A38 road can be seen the western edge of Dartmoor. *Christina Siviter*

Right above: We have now arrived at Plymouth North Road station (also on the evening of 28 May 1985). The time is just after 8pm. and No 50026 *Indomitable* has recently arrived with the 10.45 Glasgow to Penzance train, removed four coaches from this train and shunted them into the centre road. In the meantime, No 50008 *Thunderer* has been attached to the remainder of the Glasgow-Penzance train, which will then depart at 20.30 for Penzance. On the right is a Class 140 dmu on a local service, and a Class 08 shunter No 08953.

Roger Siviter

Right below: On a wet 3 April 1985, No 50011 *Centurion* runs through Devonport station, on the outskirts of Plymouth, with the 12.27 Penzance to Plymouth parcels train. *Centurion* was the first of the class to be withdrawn from service, this being on 24 February 1987.

Christina Siviter

Opposite A mile after leaving the Laira area, the line runs through Mutley tunnel and then into Plymouth North Road station. In lovely evening sunshine on 28 May 1985, No 50017 *Royal Oak* leaves North Road station behind and heads for Mutley tunnel with the 18.25 Plymouth to Paddington train, passing the site of Mutley station which lay in the cutting just before the tunnel mouth. North Road station can just be glimpsed at the back of the train as well as the signal box. Dominating the scene is the familiar station office block.

Christina Siviter

One of the great railway bridges of the world is surely Isambard Kingdom Brunel's Albert Bridge, which crosses the River Tamar between Plymouth and Saltash, and thus connects Devon and Cornwall by rail. It was opened in 1859. On 24 April 1988, Class 50 No 50023 *Howe* is seen crossing over this famous bridge with the 10.27 Penzance to Glasgow and Edinburgh, the 'Cornish Scot'. In the background is the Tamar road bridge, which was erected in 1960.

Roger Siviter

A few hundred yards west of Saltash station is Coombe viaduct, the first of over thirty major Cornish viaducts on the line to Penzance. In fact, Cornwall has more viaducts than the Settle to Carlisle route in the north of England. In pleasant winter afternoon sunshine, with the mist just beginning to descend over the River Tamar, No 50010 *Monarch* crosses Coombe viaduct with the 13.15 Penzance to Bristol van train – a very lightweight load for 2700 hp! 15 February 1988.

Roger Siviter

Opposite: Shortly after leaving Saltash, the former GWR main line to Penzance for around four miles roughly follows the course of the St Germans or Lynher River. On 17 August 1984, No 50012 *Benbow* is seen near Wearde Quay with the 09.22 Newcastle to Penzance train. This location is where the St Germans River meets the River Tamar.
Christina Siviter

Above: Our next location is the eight-arch Forder viaduct, which crosses one of the many inlets of the St Germans River – this one is called Antony Passage. It is also situated by Trematon Castle. The 07.42 Bristol Temple Meads to Penzance train with No 50015 *Valiant* in charge heads west across Forder viaduct on the morning of Thursday 5 May 1988. Trematon Castle is just off the left of the picture, and in the background is the parish church of the village of St Stephens, an area of Saltash.
Roger Siviter

Because of the curvature of the track and gradients, etc. in steam days it was not possible to have any water troughs on the Plymouth-Penzance line. Running along one of the few straight sections of track, situated between Shillingham tunnel and Lynher viaduct, is No 50007 with the 15.57 Plymouth to Penzance local train on 13 April 1988. It had earlier worked into Plymouth with the 12.27 van train from Penzance. At the rear of the train, Shillingham tunnel can be seen clearly.

Roger Siviter

A broadside view of Class 50 No 50042 *Triumph* (now preserved) as it approaches Lynher viaduct, also on 13 April 1988, with the 15.20 Plymouth to Penzance service. In the background can be seen the River Lynher and one of the many boatyards in this area. The River Lynher runs for several miles to the north of this location, its source being on the edge of Bodmin Moor.

Roger Siviter

The eight-arch Lynher viaduct which, together with Forder viaduct, was opened in 1908 after realignment of the track, provides a fine setting for No 50035 *Ark Royal* as it heads for Plymouth on Tuesday 29 May 1985 with the 09.52 Penzance to Paddington train. No 50035 is one of three Class 50s preserved by the '50 Fund' on the Severn Valley Railway, the others being Nos 50031 and 50044.

Christina Siviter

After passing through St Germans, a mile or so west of Lynher, the line runs inland towards Liskeard and crosses over the skeletal-looking Coldrenick viaduct. Coldrenick was originally an old single line timber-topped viaduct, but was rebuilt towards the end of the 1800s. On 28 August 1984, No 50018 *Resolution* crosses the viaduct with the 16.15 Penzance to Paddington train. No 50018 was one of the later 50s to be withdrawn, surviving until July 1991.

Christina Siviter

The attractive former GWR station at Menheniot (fourteen miles from Plymouth and three from Liskeard) is the setting as No 50050 *Fearless* speeds through with the 10.50 Penzance to Brighton train on 1 June 1985. Notice the neat-looking GWR waiting room and also the signal box opposite, which also controlled the adjacent goods yard, now taken up.

Roger Siviter

Above: With the ancient town of Liskeard as a backdrop, No 50017 *Royal Oak* with the 12.10 Penzance to Glasgow parcels train tackles the 1 in 79 off Bolitho viaduct as it heads east towards Plymouth. 2 May 1984. *Hugh Ballantyne*

Opposite: At 154 ft high, Liskeard viaduct, situated just east of the station, is the highest in Cornwall. It is also one of the most difficult locations to find, being in the middle of a farm – you can see it but you can't get to it! Anyway, thanks to the helpful farmer, my wife and I were able to find it and take several pictures there, including this one of No 50013 *Agincourt* crossing the viaduct with the 11.35 Penzance-Plymouth train on 29 May 1985. At the rear of the train is Liskeard station and in the valley below is the branch line to Looe, which the viaduct crosses over. *Christina Siviter*

I would not be sure, but I think this next picture must be something of a rarity in Cornwall – a double-header in Network South-East livery. On 8 April 1988, No 50025 *Invincible* and No 50003 *Temeraire* climb the 1 in 59 off Moorswater viaduct into Liskeard station. The train is the 10.27 Penzance to Edinburgh train. Note the difference in the livery at the sides of the front ends. To the right of the train can be seen the site of the west end goods yard (there was also a yard at the eastern end of the station) which also had a substantial goods shed.

Roger Siviter

This view of Moorswater viaduct was taken from near Coombe Junction and shows the line which runs to English China Clay's Moorswater driers. Behind the photographer is Coombe Junction station where Liskeard to Looe trains reverse, etc. No 50013 crosses the graceful Moorswater viaduct on 29 May 1985 with the 15.05 Plymouth to Penzance local train. Also note the piers of the original timber-built viaduct.   *Christina Siviter*

Above: From Doublebois, some four miles west of Liskeard, the line follows the valley of the River Fowey for the next nine miles to Lostwithiel. For up trains this means a long climb of around six miles, with grades as steep as 1 in 65. No 50149 tops the summit of that climb near the site of Doublebois station with the 14.55 St Blazey to Gloucester goods train on 11 April 1988.   *Roger Siviter*

Opposite: The route through the Fowey Valley, or Glynn Valley as it is known locally, crosses over quite a few viaducts, including Derrycombe viaduct where on 1 June 1985 No 50041 *Bulwark* is photographed heading for Plymouth with the 09.55 Penzance to Leeds train. In the background are the southern slopes of Bodmin Moor.   *Christina Siviter*

On 15 September 1983 No 50045 *Achillies* is caught by the autumn sunshine as it leaves Bodmin Road station (from 1984 known as Bodmin Parkway) and heads up the heavily wooded Glynn Valley with the 12.10 Penzance to Glasgow parcels train. Bodmin Road was the junction for the GWR line to Bodmin and also Boscarne junction, where it connected with the LSWR lines to Wenford and Wadebridge. After closure, the line between Bodmin Parkway and Bodmin (and also Boscarne junction) was preserved and became known as the Bodmin & Wenford Railway, with regular trains between Bodmin Parkway and the old Bodmin General station. The line to Bodmin can be seen on the right hand side of the train.

Hugh Ballantyne

No 50044 *Exeter* and No 50018 *Resolution* climb the 1 in 65 into Bodmin Parkway station on 30 May 1985 with the 10.24 Penzance to Birmingham New Street train. On the right hand side is the line to Bodmin General and also sidings, all now part of the Bodmin & Wenford Railway. *Christina Siviter*

Above: The three miles or so between Bodmin Parkway and Lostwithiel, the line runs through pleasant farming land which fringes on Bodmin Moor. On a bright early spring day – 15 February 1988 – No 50010 *Monarch* heads the 06.45 Swindon to Penzance train through Newton, a mile from Bodmin Parkway station.

Roger Siviter

Opposite: Looking round from the previous picture, we see No 50012 *Benbow* heading north on the 4 May 1988 with the 12.20 Penzance to Glasgow parcels train. This location is also just north of Brownqueen tunnel. The Penzance to Glasgow van train was a regular working for the Class 50s but was not always loaded to thirteen vehicles as on this occasion.

Hugh Ballantyne

In smart external condition, No 50030 *Repulse* swings round the reverse curves at Restormel and approaches Lostwithiel (where it is due to stop for passengers) with the 15.57 Plymouth to Penzance local train. The field on the left hand side is now part of Lostwithiel Golf Course, which has been built in the last few years on the farmland which covered this area.

Roger Siviter

With a hint of rain in the air, *Royal Oak* rounds the tight curve at the northern end of Lostwithiel station and heads for Plymouth with the 10.24 Penzance to Birmingham and Liverpool on 31 May 1984. At the rear of the train can be seen the neat-looking station, complete with signal box, which not only controls the semaphore signalling but also the level crossing just in front of the box. Notice also the row of tented china clay wagons, Lostwithiel being the junction for Carne Point (on the former branch line to Fowey) from where the china clay is shipped. Also on the right hand side is the milk depot with a row of milk tankers, probably bound for the London area.

Christina Siviter

The Lostwithiel area still possesses some very nice GWR semaphore signals with perhaps none better than this bracket signal, situated at the end of the down platform. On 10 April 1988, No 50018 *Resolution* approaches Lostwithiel station where it is about to stop, with the 09.11 Penzance to Plymouth local train. On the right hand side of the train was a goods yard and goods shed (now demolished) and on the left, between the bracket signal and the notice, can be seen the start of the branch to Carne Point and also the china clay sidings.

Roger Siviter

This picture was taken about half a mile west of Lostwithiel station and shows refurbished Class 50 No 50001 (but still in old livery) heading west for Par with the 09.20 Brighton to Penzance train on 17 September 1983. In the background can be seen the town of Lostwithiel and on the right hand side the milk depot.

Hugh Ballantyne

Opposite: Having passed through Treverrin tunnel, No 50004 *St Vincent* speeds along near Treesmill, just east of Par, with the 13.30 Birmingham New Street to Penzance train on 31 May 1985. Notice the wild rhododendrons which abound in Cornwall in the late spring and early summer.   *Christina Siviter*

Above: On 28 August 1984, No 50001 *Dreadnought*, now in 'large logo' livery, approaches Par with the 13.40 Paddington to Penzance train. Like Lostwithiel, Par still retains its signal box and semaphore signalling.   *Christina Siviter*

No 50028 *Tiger* pauses at Par station on the 27 April 1984 with the 11.55 Penzance to Plymouth train. To the right of platform two can be seen the lines which not only lead to St Blazey shed and yard (a short distance from Par station) but also form the start of the lengthy branch line to Newquay, situated on Cornwall's north coast, some twenty miles from Par. Also in the distance, on the left hand side, can be seen the chimneys of the clay drying plant at Par Harbour. Notice also the GWR platform canopies over the platforms and over the station entrance, as well as the breakdown train.

Roger Siviter

At 5.20 p.m. on the evening of Saturday 22 August 1987, No 50034 *Furious* rounds the corner from St Blazey and approaches Par station with the 16.28 Newquay to Wolverhampton train. At the time, these were known in the timetable as Holidaymaker Express trains. 1987 was the last summer of locomotive-hauled trains to Newquay, the last working being a special train on Sunday 4 October, the 08.25 from Paddington and return, hauled by No 50034 and No 50035. To the left of the signal box is the main line, which is also joined by the loop line on the right hand side.

Roger Siviter

Our next location is the old Cornish town of St Austell, just under five miles west of Par. On 27 April 1984, *Royal Oak* (No 50017) pauses at St Austell station with the up midday parcels train, the 12.20 Penzance to Glasgow. Worthy of note are the ex-GWR platform building and the splendid station footbridge. For many years, St Austell station was the terminus for the motor-rail trains which ran into Cornwall from various parts of the country. But as can be seen from this picture, this would not be for much longer, because the workmen were already beginning to dismantle the sidings, etc. which were used for this service. The sidings were not completely removed but truncated, leaving two short spur sidings at the eastern end of the up platform for shunting purposes, which still remain today.

Roger Siviter

This picture was taken at St Austell a few months after the previous scene, on 31 August 1984, and shows the area where the motor-rail sidings were, now used for car parking. Heading into the station on that sunny August day is No 50037 *Illustrious* in charge of the 16.15 Penzance to Paddington train. This photograph gives a closer view of the footbridge and also shows the GWR logo which is emblazoned into it. No 50037 was one of the last Class 50s to be withdrawn. It was taken out of service on 9 September 1991. *Christina Siviter*

Halfway between Penzance and Saltash, and two miles west of St Austell, is Burngullow, junction for the now freight-only lines to Drinnick Mill and Parkandillack. On 29 May 1985, No 50047 *Swiftsure* climbs past the old station house (the station closed in 1931) with the 16.35 Plymouth to Penzance train.

On the left hand side can be seen the sidings for the nearby Blackpool clay driers, with a solitary tented china clay wagon on show. The main line was singled in the autumn of 1986, when the down line was taken out between Burngullow and Probus – six miles to the west of here. *Christina Siviter*

This picture, taken at Burngullow on 18 September 1981, shows No 50006 *Neptune* and No 50045 *Achilles* passing the junction for Drinnick Mill and Parkandillack with the 13.45 Penzance to Plymouth parcels train. This picture shows well the old and new liveries prevailing at the time on refurbished locomotives. Note the GWR signal box, which also controlled the junction. It closed in 1986 with the singling of the line, and was then used as a PW hut.

Hugh Ballantyne

After the china clay area around St Austell and Burngullow, for the next eleven miles the line runs through farming land before reaching Cornwall's only city – Truro. Several viaducts are crossed in this eleven miles, including Coombe St Stephen. This viaduct passes over a tributary of the River Fal and is roughly three miles west of Burngullow. On 22 April 1988, No 50035, now in Network South-East livery and with axle-boxes painted yellow, runs over the ten-arch viaduct with the 12.27 Penzance to Plymouth van train. On the left of the viaduct can be seen the piers of the original Brunel viaduct.

Roger Siviter

Two miles from Truro is the very pleasant rural area of Buckshead. No 50033 *Glorious* has just left Buckshead tunnel and is speeding downgrade in warm spring sunshine toward St Austell and Plymouth with the 15.25 up local train from Penzance. The date is the 5 April 1988. This train is due to arrive in Plymouth at 17.31, taking just over two hours for the 79½ mile journey, which includes twelve stops.

Christina Siviter

Last of the class, No 50050 *Fearless*, pulls into Truro at just after 7 p.m. on the evening of 30 May 1984 with the 13.40 ('Jumbo' train) Paddington to Penzance service. The locomotive is framed between the GWR signal box and a GWR semaphore signal. Also, above the first coach can be seen the spire of Truro Cathedral.

Christina Siviter

Truro station possesses two GWR footbridges, as can be seen in this picture of No 50031 *Hood* as it pauses at the station with the 08.55 Penzance to Birmingham New Street and Newcastle train on 30 May 1985. In the mid 1980s, the Railway in Cornwall became known as Cornish Railways, with a special logo on the Class 37s from St Blazey shed which worked the china clay trains. The building on the right hand side is the office for the manager of Cornish Railways. Also, part of the logo can be seen to the left of the blade of the semaphore signal. Truro is also the junction for the branch line to Falmouth, to the south of the Cathedral city.   *Roger Siviter*

The next fifteen miles or so from Truro, the line runs through the industrial and the former tin mining area of Cornwall. At Chacewater, six miles west of Truro, was the Blue Circle Cement terminal. On 30 May 1984, No 50013 rounds the curve past the disused Chacewater station and the cement depot with the 10.18 Paddington to Penzance train. The depot closed in the late 1980s. At the rear of the train can be seen Blackwater (or Chacewater) viaduct. Just west of here was the junction for the branch line to Perranporth and Newquay, which closed in the early 1960s.   *Christina Siviter*

Left: On the morning of 31 August 1984, No 50022 *Anson* climbs past the famous engine house at Scorrier, just north of Redruth, with the 10.50 Penzance to Paddington train. This engine house was known as Hallenbeagle, and is probably the most well known in the area – certainly to railway enthusiasts. Scorrier was also the start of the tin mining area of Redruth and Camborne. *Christina Siviter*

Opposite: Just north of Redruth were Drump Lane sidings where, on 30 May 1985, No 50050 hurries by with the 15.05 Plymouth to Penzance train. Of latter years, these sidings were used by Chacewater cement trains for run-round purposes. In the background can be seen St Agnes Beacon, some 628 ft high.
Christina Siviter

We leave the industrial area of Cornwall behind us and rejoin the seaside at Hayle, some seven miles from Penzance. On the early evening of 5 May 1988, No 50036 *Victorious* crosses the 227 yard long Hayle viaduct with the 15.20 Plymouth to Penzance train. At the rear of the train can be seen Hayle station.

I use the term 'seaside' rather loosely here because in fact Hayle was an important port in the area, with a harbour and a wharf from which there was a line to the station which closed around 1981. There was also a power station at Hayle, which also closed in 1981.

Hugh Ballantyne

What was then the new A30 Hayle bypass gives a good view of up trains as can be seen in this picture taken of No 50020 *Revenge* as it heads for Plymouth on 6 May 1988 with the 09.11 local train from Penzance. In the background can be seen the small town of St Erth, with the signal box and station just visible. At this point the line is crossing over the River Hayle, which runs into Hayle Harbour and then into St Ives Bay. *Roger Siviter*

Left: Our next location is St Erth, which is also the junction for the holiday and artistic town of St Ives, for years the home of many famous painters and sculptors, and the New Tate Gallery. At around 7.40 p.m. on the evening of 30 May 1985, No 50013 waits to leave St Erth with the 19.27 postal train off Penzance. This travelling post office (TPO) contains letter boxes built into the sides of the coaches for the public to post their letters, etc. One of these boxes can be seen just to the right of the signal pole. The St Ives branch platform is just left of the railings, and this line connects up with the line leaving the main line and running to the left of the signal box.

Roger Siviter

Oposite: This view of St Erth station (from the west) was taken on the evening of 5 May 1988, and shows No 50036 as it is about to stop at the station with the 15.20 Plymouth to Penzance train. This picture also shows the lovely GWR footbridge and station buildings complete with canopies, and also the signal box and the junction to St Ives. By way of a remarkable coincidence, and unknown to Hugh Ballantyne and myself until the preparation of this book, this is the same train as seen on Hayle viaduct.

Roger Siviter

No 50004 *St Vincent* passes Long Rock Depot at Penzance on the evening of
30 May 1985 with the 13.40 Paddington to Penzance train. On the right hand
side is St Michael's Mount, which is accessible from the shore when the tide is
out.

Roger Siviter

We have now arrived at Penzance where, on the early evening of 5 April 1988, No 50004 *St Vincent* arrives at this south-westerly terminus of the former GWR with the 15.57 local train off Plymouth, while looking on is No 50012 *Benbow* with the 19.27 up postal train. This view shows the main line as it runs through Long Rock (the site of the locomotive depot) and out to Marazion. The blue waters of Mount's Bay complete this historic scene. *Christina Siviter*

Above: On the evening of 5 May 1988, No 50031 *Hood* waits to leave Penzance station with the 18.30 to Bristol Temple Meads. It had earlier worked in with the 15.57 from Plymouth. In the outer platform is the up postal waiting to leave at 19.27 behind No 50036 *Victorious*. Notice also the Class 08 shunter No 08801. Dominating the skyline is St Mary's church.

Roger Siviter